CUSTOM
MERCEDES-BENZ

CUSTOM MERCEDES-BENZ

DAVID SPARROW AND ADRIENNE KESSEL

First published in Great Britain in 1995
by Osprey, an imprint of Reed Consumer
Books Limited, Michelin House,
81 Fulham Road, London SW3 6RB and
Auckland, Melbourne, Singapore and Toronto.

ISBN 185532 517 9

Project Editor Shaun Barrington
Editors Iain Ayre and Jane Northey
Page design Paul Kime
Printed in Hong Kong

This book is dedicated to David and Vivienne Wood

**With grateful thanks to:
H Niemann, Paul Ffolkes-Halbard, Franz Maag, Carley Kaufengerer, Dieter Ritter, Luise Layher, Marcel van Schaik, Mercedes-Benz at Unterturkheim, Mercedes GB, Porsche at Zuffenhausen, Philippe Zucker at AMG, Dirk Manuel Lohrbach at Brabus, Philippe Fontaine at Duchatelet, Duncan Smith at Lancaster Styling, Willy Mosselman at Mosselman Turbo Systems, Jon Bolton at Rude Mercedes, the Staff at Gockel, R Stauba at Rusta, Wolfgang Krause at KLS, J Lang at Eris, the staff at Lorinser, everyone at Sound Science, Adrian Towland at Path Group. Thanks also to Jeremy Walton for invaluable additional information.**

The photos were all taken on Leica R6
Cameras with Leica lenses ranging from
16mm to 560mm, all housed in a bag
especially made by the good folk at
Billingham.

DIRK HAFEMEISTER
RUDOLF SCHENKER
MATTHIAS JABS
FRANZ BECKENBAUER
Wir fahren ab
BERLI
200

Contents

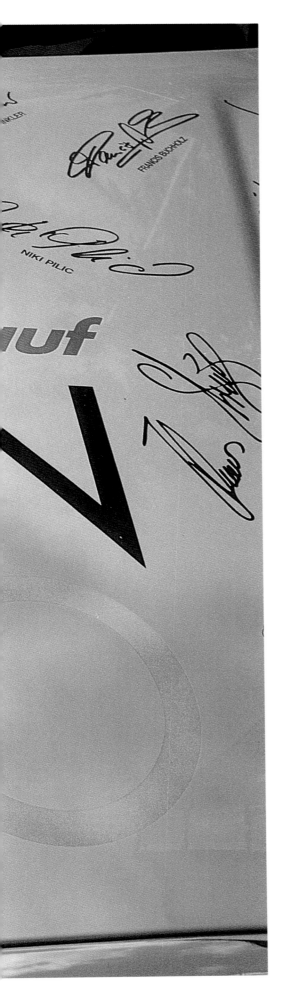

Left

German personalities, and sportsmen including the legendary Franz Beckenbauer, signed in support on the Mercedes Benz-backed Berlin 2000 celebrations. The signatures were employed on road and race cars of 1993

Introduction

Why take a piece of brilliant engineering, a well-made quality motor car of pedigree and taste, and change it?

Is it not gilding the lily? Are there not enough examples of the internal combustion engine, clothed in an infinite number of forms, to please every taste?

No, there are not. Fortunately for the motor industry, there are as many different opinions on what constitutes the perfect automobile as there are customers. Were it not so, then car showrooms would be small, discreet affairs with 'countryside-view' calendars on the walls, accessory shops would sell only oil and how-to-mend-it manuals, and the ubiquitous motoring magazines would have trouble filling their glossy pages at all. Of course, not all of the reasons for changing the character of one's motor car are frivolous, and there are very sound reasons for wanting to optimise the performance, comfort and appointments of a car, whatever it may be.

Let us leave aside the tired, overused pseudo-psychological nonsense. Let us not be sidetracked by talk of car worship and religion-substitutes. We are talking real people here, men and women with the ability and desire to make rational decisions based on their needs and lifestyles. A person's company car allowance may be generous enough

In essence, all early cars from the venerable Daimler Benz company are 'customised', that is, tailored to the specific needs of the customer: and particularly those produced for heads of state and royalty, as so many were. Prince Heinrech at the wheel of a 24hp Benz in 1905, a phaeton. The Prince is credited with introducing automotives within the Imperial Family, the Hohezollerns, and also, by some sources, for the invention of the windshield wiper in 1908

With Victor Hèmery at the wheel, the 'Lightning-Benz' set a world record at Brooklands in 1909 with a speed of 202.69km/h. The car, which now resides in the Daimler-Benz museum, showed its full potential at Daytona Beach, setting a record speed of 211.8 km/h over a mile from a flying start. The record of 228.1km/h which the car set in 1911 remained unbroken for eight years

happened. Their products had two major advantages: They were competitively priced, and the quality was of the highest.

The three-pointed star device which became the Mercedes emblem was introduced by the Daimler company in 1909, to represent the three elements in which their engines were used – in the air, in the water, and on land. The emblem of Benz & Cie contained a laurel wreath surrounding the word 'Benz'. The merged company chose as its badge the star, surrounded by two sections of laurel wreath and the words 'Mercedes Benz'. Immediately after the merger, two models for day-to-day motoring and one luxury model were introduced to the market. Benz had retired from active service in his company in 1903, but had continued as a director and adviser. He continued in this capacity in the newly merged firm until his death in April 1929. His life had spanned the dawn of the age of motoring, its infancy and its growth to maturity. His legacy is with us to this day.

Above

Dr Ferdinand Porsche developed the SSK – SS for Super Sport, K for kurtz (=short) from the earlier supercharged models, with sports car racing in mind. The Mercedes team won an impressive string of victories with the cars between 1929 and 1931. In 1930, Rudolf Caracciola won the European Sports Car Championship in an SSK. The car's 7068cc engine developed 170hp without supercharger, and 225hp with. Top speed was 192km/h

Right

The 500K was an elegant sporting car, built between 1934 and 1936, which combined good performance with a high level of creature comfort. The five-litre engine produced 100hp in standard form, 160hp with the supercharger attached. This car is a special bodied, four-door Streamliner saloon. The rear end curves dramatically, and the rear wheels are covered. There are only two of these Mercedes in existence

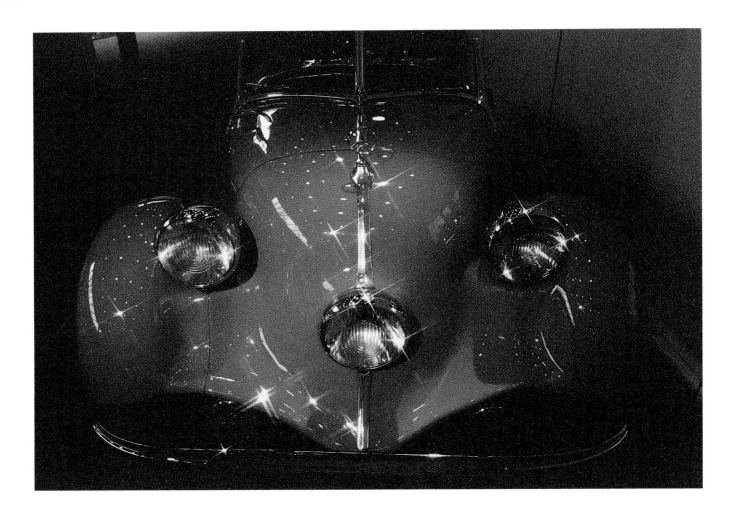

Above

Unusual styling for this Mercedes-Benz 150 Sports convertible
from 1935. The rear-engined design of the car failed to gain
acceptance at Daimler-Benz, and production was halted in
1938. The car had a 1500cc engine and was capable of
140km/h

Right

The origins of the Daimler-Benz Museum at Untertürkheim
are to be found in the earliest days of the automobile; items
were preserved by both Daimler and Benz from the word go,
the former exhibiting cars and components as early as 1911.
The first bona fide auto museum was set up by Daimler-Benz
in 1936 to mark half a century of manufacture. A new, much
larger museum was built in 1961, to be completely refurbished
in time to be opened as part of the centenary celebrations in
1986. In addition to examples of the many milestones in automobile evolution to the present day, the museum features
buses, aeroplanes, boats – and agricultural/utility vehicles –
every facet of the Daimler-Benz story

Above right

The 600 Limousines were built on a separate production line
which was dedicated to them alone. This allowed the incorpo-
ration of the many options and features which made the car
so special. The car was powered by a 6332cc fuel-injected V8
engine. The long wheelbase version could boast six doors if
required. In 1965, the most productive year for the car, just
345 units were built. The 600 was in demand from heads of
state all over the world as an exclusive saloon for official occa-
sions. By 1974, with world oil production crises and European
financial problems, production had dropped to 25 annually,
and ceased completely in 1981. Over two and a half thousand
had been built in all

Top

The AMG 'manufaktur' service upholsters and trims interiors in a wide range of materials and finishes; more than a dozen different leathers and a variety of woods are available. Cars can also be built entirely to the customer's specification – every one unique, but all to the Mercedes standard. AMG are particulary effective at meeting series production taste, their 3.6 litre C-class selling by the thousand in the mid-nineties and setting new international standards

Above and left

AMG began life in an old mill at Burgstall, moving to new premises in Affalterbach in 1976. A second factory was opened in 1985. In addition, there are six regional AMG centres in Germany, situated at the corresponding Mercedes dealerships, with AMG specialists in attendance. AMG Mercedes performance cars or individual alterations are sold at home and overseas (especially Asia, UK, mainland Europe and South America) through the 4500-strong Mercedes networks, carrying full Mercedes warranty. AMG standards must of course be Mercedes standards

Above

The workforce at AMG has grown steadily over the past ten years, from 100 in 1987, 200 in 1989 to 350 in 1983. Needless to say, this number includes many highly-trained specialists and technicians. By the start of 1995 AMG had more than doubled initial sales forecasts for their complete C36 version of C-class and anticipated selling up to 5000 converted C-class, including individual, suspension, styling and wheels packs

Left

AMG's sporting development and that of its production cars influence each other to the benefit of both. At the heart of AMG's growth has been the basic engines engineering skills that echoed founder Hans Werner Aufrecht's former employment at Daimler Benz. The Affalterbach site housed 400 people in 1995, plus all the facilities that are needed to offer a 7.2 litre V12 to the S-class captains of industry or to create, build and brake-test a racing V6 engine from an original 8-cyclinder production car design

were unveiled in Geneva. The racing version of the car incorporated a complex roll-cage to stiffen the frame and increase the rigidity, although the suspension remained largely unmodified. To save on weight, the interior of the car was gutted. Carbon fibre and Kevlar reinforced plastic were used for bonnet, boot lid and tail. The fuel tank was replaced by a 110 litre racing version which was situated in the spare wheel compartment. From 1991, AMG were responsible for developing, preparing and maintaining Mercedes competition project cars. AMG products are sold through the world-wide dealer network of Mercedes themselves.

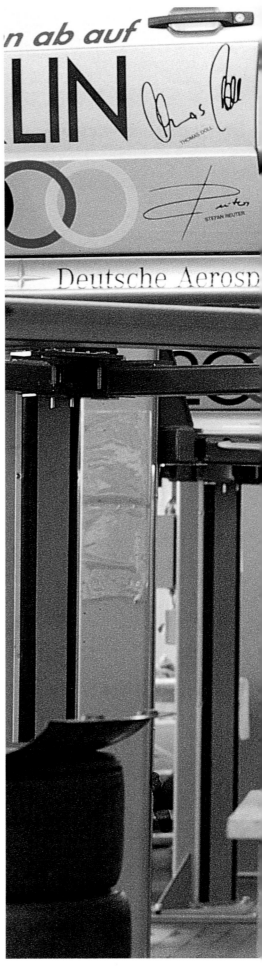

Above

This AMG special edition styling 'Berlin 2000' is covered with the signatures of many personalities, sporting and otherwise. These strictly limited — and therefore highly prized — custom editions died with the 190E and the arrival of C-class

Right

Here are the 1993 racing equivalents of the road car. They had 380 bhp from uprated versions of the 2.5/16 DOHC 16-valve motor, rode on magnesium wheels from 18 inch diameters upward over enormous disc brakes and race-fabricated suspension that gave the ultimate 'Low Rider' track stance. Even more creditably, these racers were equipped with road-relevant developments of electronic anti-lock braking (ABS), steering wheel airbag and power steering, plus the catalytic convertors that German racing demanded. There are three distinct AMG lines. Firstly, the technology package, which increases engine output. It also includes a sport exhaust system, upgraded brakes and Mercedes sports suspension. The second option is visual styling, which is available for all Mercedes except the 500E. The third choice comprises AMG sport suspension, plus wheels and tyres. Naturally there are numerous mix and match possibilities too!

Above

AMG participated in motor sport for the first time in 1971, and were victorious with their 428hp 300 SEL 6.3 litre AMG-Mercedes. In 1988 they entered the German Touring Car Championships as the official partner of Mercedes-Benz for the first time

Left

In 1992, AMG driver Klaus Ludwig won the German Touring Car Championship in a 190 E2.5 Evolution 2, with Mercedes taking the manufacturers' trophy and AMG the team cup. 1994 saw the debut of the C-class in the championship; victory came in only the second race of the season, at Hockenheim, and was speedily followed by further wins

Overleaf

AMG-Mercedes had their revenge on Alfa Romeo's 4x4 155s in the 1994 German Championship. AMG's beautifully crafted current interpretations of the 'Silver Arrows' colours wre the most radically developed rear drive racing saloons in the world. Here is 1994 Champion Klaus Ludwig, who immediately left for Opel. No matter, the AMG-Mercedes kept winning in 1995…(Photo courtesy Jeremy Walton)

Brabus

Brabus are another German firm to concentrate upon an amazing cross-section of services for the individual customer. They are not a racing-orientated company, but are particularly good at blending the qualities that provide civilised road car speed. Directed by Bodo Buschmann from spacious showroom/workshop premises at Bottrop, Brabus was founded as part of the 35-year-old Buschmann group. They sell their Mercedes customers anything from a scale model to white heat engine technology for a faster road car. The company does not restrict its efforts to the more popular – and affordable – 190E or C-classes, catering for the six-cylinder middleweights as well as the off-road *Geländerwagen*. Brabus were one of the early instigators of the 24-valve technology for the six cylinder units; and are also capable of enlarging both the inline sixes and the V8s with replacement crankshafts to order. They are prominent in the aerodynamics body kit market, providers of thoroughly overhauled wood and leather interiors and have their own ranges of fine alloy wheels for that final, distinctive touch.

Brabus believe that there are certain aspects of their creations that will inevitably never be seen or fully appreciated. The many hours of research and development, experimentation and testing, for example, which take place behind the scenes. Their prospective purchasers expect their cars to cover hundreds of thousands of miles without unacceptable expense, so that background work is a very important part of the equation. As Brabus cars are sold all around the world, tests have been undertaken running the cars at full throttle with the radiator half-covered, in order to simulate the temperature conditions that the cars may have to contend with.

New materials have altered the methods of construction of the skirts and aerodynamic panels. Formerly constructed of handrolled sheets expertly cut and glued together, they are now manufactured from PUR-Rim, a plastic material with properties which make it ideal for making preformed construction units. Traditional materials have their place too, of course; interiors are usually to be found in soft

Above

Brabus head of research and development, engineer Ullrich Gauffrès with the twelve-cylinder dream machine of his design. He has the utmost respect for the original; many months of intense work on the part of Herr Gauffrès and his team has ensured the integrity of the finished work of art

Top

Before he began customising Mercedes cars, Frederic Duchatelet ran a vehicle body workshop, which he founded in 1968

Above

Duchatelet invest a great deal of time and money in training for specialist skills. It takes two years, for example, to train someone to the point where they can work unsupervised on the leather trimming of the dashboard

Right

The complete mobile office; for the businessman who spends much of his day travelling between appointments. Phones, faxes, space to work, the ability to stretch out and relax too. In the limos proper, passenger and driver are separated by a screen

Above

All the leather and suede that Duchatelet use if of the highest quality. Consequently it is also very fine, and not easy to work. As it is also very expensive, craftsmanship must be of the highest standards, and wastage kept to the minimum

Right

Quality is the keyword at Duchatelet, and the control of quality is very stringent; checking is rigorous, and if any fault is found, no stone is left unturned. Not just whole boxes, but the entire pallets will be opened up and checked if necessary

Duchatelet set great store by their workers; it is important that those people who are working on a car actually have some feeling for it, that they take pride in their own productivity. In addition to bespoke automobile creations, the company is also involved in the interior design and fitment of medium-sized aircraft through their Executive Aviation Department. Where, no doubt, the same company ethos holds sway

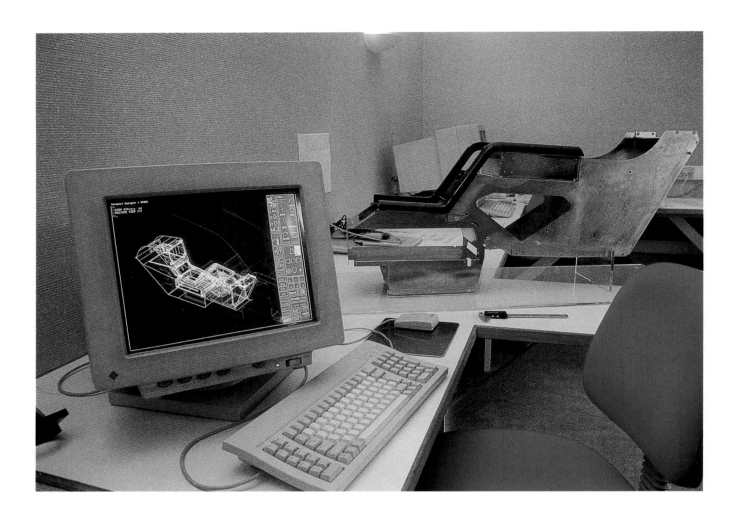

Above

Computer-aided design plays an important part in the development process.
Duchatelet also have a security division which designs and builds custom armoured
modifications and high-level protection

Right

All accessories are marketed under the Carat banner; these include wheels and
spoilers on the outside, consoles and wood trim on the inside

The Duchatelet workshops are a model of tidiness and order. The level of expertise is high and time is carefully managed

Wood kits are marketed under the Carat Accessories name. Again, they are manufactured to the high standards laid down by Mercedes themselves, and distributed across seventeen countries by importers carefully selected for the purpose

Mosselman

Mosselman Turbo Systems was established in 1974 in California, the major centre at that time for the turbo- and supercharging of cars. Four years later, the company moved to The Netherlands. Owner Willy Mosselman has travelled extensively, gathering information from Europe, from the USA, from the Middle East and the Far East. As a result he has developed systems that can happily be driven flat out all day. There is a Mosselman system to suit most Mercedes models, including the diesels.

Mosselman's home market of The Netherlands is a good example of how expectations have changed over the last few years. In the relatively prosperous late eighties, large and expensive motor cars abounded. Fuel consumption was of little interest. Then times got harder. A swingeing tax was introduced on the purchase of a car, with another tax to be paid for personal use of a company vehicle. The bigger and more expensive the car, the more massive the tax bill. Suddenly, the big cars started to go. Everyone wanted the smallest car they could tolerate; mid-range cars enjoyed a boom. Purchasers then turned their attentions to increasing the power of these cars – and that is where Mosselman found a new market for turbo systems.

There is a similar situation in the Far East. The top marque European cars such as Mercedes are in demand, but only a low-powered version will be imported, or assembled locally. Add your three passengers, switch on the air-conditioning, and potentially you have a struggling powerplant. There may be enormous traffic jams, but it is embarrassing to have your luxury European car outdone at the traffic lights by a standard Honda Civic. Cities throughout the world are grinding to a halt: it is no longer possible to drive fast on a day-to-day basis. So the emphasis inevitably shifts from the big, fast, race car manqué to the smaller, cheaper-to-run car, and the power problem is solved with a turbo system.

Mosselman Turbo Systems are produced at Arkel, near Rotterdam, and shipped all over the world. The company has a network of trained and approved fitters worldwide. The units, which can usually be fitted in one day, do not interfere with any of the options available from

Mosselman produce ten different turbo and four different supercharging systems, with new units being developed continuously as manufacturers' models change. In addition to Mercedes, the company also supply systems that fit other marques, including BMW and Range Rover

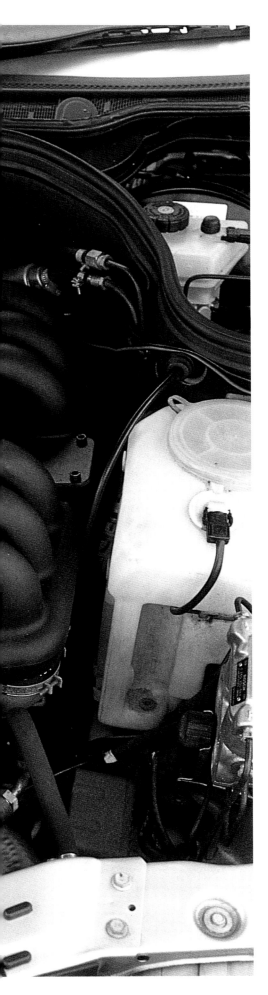

Mercedes themselves. In the event of the car being sold, the unit can be removed and fitted to a replacement vehicle. Mosselman believes that engines modified in the normal way tend to produce additional horsepower only at high revs, at the expense of torque at low revs. This often makes for a noisy engine, rough idling and high fuel consumption. He aims for high torque at low revs, aligned with proper management of fuel systems, superior quality of materials and attention to detail.

Above

However stylish the exterior, it is what goes on under the bonnet that is of prime importance in the Mosselman philosophy

Left

One of the many important criteria for Mosselman's systems is that they should not compromise the integrity of the original engine. They should be able to be removed completely, returning the engine to its original status

Above

Window of opportunity; Mosselman's system boosts the performance to the level of Mercedes' own 16 valve Cosworth version – 186hp with 0 to 100km/h in 7.8 seconds. Fuel consumption remains good, with reasonably careful driving, at over 25mpg (10km/litre)

Above right

The rear wing is manufactured from epoxy-covered Kevlar for strength

Right

Stone-chip-proof covering on the headlamp glass helps prevent expensive and dangerous breakages

Above

Willy Mosselman has over twenty years of experience in the field of turbo and super-charging. He has travelled extensively, and has detailed knowledge of the differing needs of customers in Europe, USA and the Near and Far East

Right

High torque at low revs; this is the goal that Mosselman aim for with their systems. In this way, the all-round driveability of the car is improved, accepting that the vast majority of customers want a reliable car that drives well in the real world, rather than racing-driver dreamland

Above

From the company headquarters in the Netherlands, kits are shipped throughout the world and fitted by technicians trained specifically by Mosselman. Most units can be fitted by them within the course of a day. Mercedes guarantees are not invalidated by the additions

Left

The interior of one of Willy Mosselman's own cars, revealing a dedicated, enthusiastic driver; electronically adjustable seats, smart but practical leather, trimmed kickplates and a sports gearstick

kits comprising spoiler and side sills, plus extras such as colour-coded
wheels and sports tyres. The company also runs a 190 cabriolet of their
own design, for which decent summers, or Jamaican ones, would be
appreciated. 'Rude' of course can mean solid and well-made, which Jon's
cars undoubtedly are: however we can be certain that the customer
had the 'impolite' definition in mind when he coined that name!

Above

*Strange as it may seem, this photograph was taken in the depths of winter. But does
it look cold? No, these cars definitely have inbuilt warming properties. Facetious jour-
nalists have suggested that the rear wing would double as a first-rate barbecue table*

Left

*Getting ruder – full body styling based on Mercedes' own Evolution 2, including the
amazing adjustable rear wing and rear window shroud. Rude Mercs improved the
suspension to suit*

Above

Strangely, although Rude Mercedes customs are more extreme than most, the recognisable Mercedes-ness is still there, and this is not as true with some of the more subtle body-styling efforts. Jamaican colours for the head-restraints in hand-stitched leather, same colours on the steering wheel

Right

What would Herr Daimler have thought of all this? Would Herr Jellinek have allowed his daughter to go out in one?

Overleaf

The Evolution 3 bodykit combines four wide arches, front and rear bumper spoilers, side sills, door panels, adjustable Evolution rear wing, rear window shroud and SEC-style bonnet

Top

Black leather everywhere, all outlined with outrageous canary yellow piping. Less well-made and it would just look expensively cheap, but Jon Bolton is not a man to do things by halves; his way, it all looks expensively flamboyant

Above

Brakes: standard disks with ABS. Wheels: colour coded 9 x 17 inch RG design wheels with 245/35 ZR17 Dunlop Sport D40 tyres. Suspension: Sachs motorsport shock absorbers all round with Lorinser coil springs

Left

Engine: Mercedes Cosworth 2.3 litre 16V enlarged to 2.5 litre, fully lightened and balanced. Modified cylinder head with sports cams. Modified injection system and ECU. Tubular exhaust manifold, three inch exhaust system. Uprated five speed Getrag 'box

As this is a car whose engine is capable of 400hp, you're more likely to see it from behind; and you'll recognise it easily — it's yellow, and it's RUDE!

Above

Göckel provide styling and accessories for many Mercedes models; one of their products is called the '500E look' This provides everything to make your base-model appear more exciting

Left

The Göckel trademark features the company name, and behind it a representation of the Mercedes star in 'Starship Enterprise' perspective. This is a car that boldly goes

A Göckel car shows off its highly distinctive style; it really is a body that puffs out its chest at you, like an inappropriately dressed rally car

On a more practical level, Göckel offer electric windows, automatic door closing and alarm systems — essential if you intend packing in other goodies from the shelves

Above

From black tail-lamps, replacement grilles, foglights, headlamp washers, alloy wheels, gear shift knobs, fascia panels...

Left

...to complete styling kits, sports suspension and exhausts

Overleaf

Göckel interiors can be trimmed in leather, with colours both garish and refined to choose from. Here the whole dashboard is trimmed and stitched in leather. The steering wheel boss wears the company logo

500E

The 500E was a unique Mercedes; it was manufactured by Porsche at their factory in Stuttgart. Porsche were involved in the car's conception too. However this was not the first time that the paths of these two automotive personalities had crossed.

In 1923, Ferdinand Porsche joined the Daimler organisation in Stuttgart as technical director. He was the prime mover behind the big sports racing cars that Mercedes produced in the twenties, including the 6.8 litre S and 7.1 litre SS and SSK. Porsche's tenure at Daimler was not a smooth ride however, and he left after five years with the company and returned to Austria. But Porsche did not sever the Daimler connection completely. By 1931 he was in business by himself, and working alongside former Mercedes colleague Adolf Rosenberger to produce the successful Auto-Union racing cars. Three years later, Porsche had produced the prototype of his 'People's Car'.

A batch of thirty early Beetles was manufactured by Daimler- Benz. The company then worked with Porsche on building a car with which to launch an assault upon the world land-speed record at Salt Lake; this was the Porsche Daimler Super Automobil. Unfortunately, the car never managed to try for the record. When war broke out, it was still on a boat crossing the Atlantic Ocean. It now resides in the Daimler Benz museum.

An area of Porsche's Zuffenhausen factory was set aside purely for the production of the Mercedes 500E. Those working on the project had been specially trained in the ways of Mercedes, in order that the company's particular standards were adhered to. Only twelve of the five-litre V8 engines were built each day, with annual production being just two and a half thousand, over a hundred of which were destined for the UK market. The 326bhp 500E is the fastest accelerating road-going car that Mercedes have ever produced; zero to 62mph takes just

Made in Stuttgart until 1993, the Mercedes 500E, which was hand-built at the Porsche factory in Zuffenhausen, just a few miles down the road from the Mercedes-Benz plant

5.9 seconds. The engine is managed by an ingenious electronic control system, and is governed not to exceed 156mph, no matter how much the accelerator is depressed. Because the car had so much power, an acceleration skid control device was a standard fitting. Sensors detect the faintest beginnings of rear-wheel spin or loss of grip, and the throttle is automatically limited, while progressive braking is applied to correct the situation. A sophisticated communications system amasses large amounts of data from the various sensors in a very short time, so the car's control systems are in touch with each other constantly. The 500E's standard equipment is lavish, including a quality four-speaker stereo system, air conditioning, sports seats throughout, cruise control, electric seat controls in front, central locking and walnut veneer panels.

Above

Build quality and production control were of equal importance to Mercedes and Porsche. Both companies have a reputation for the high level of training that their staff undergo. The Porsche craftsmen building the 500E have in addition been versed in the particular priorities of Mercedes

Left

Part of the Porsche factory was set aside to build the 500E, only in LHD. The car set new standards for silent speed and is undoubtedly destined for classic status

Above

Ferdinand Porsche was at one time head of design at Daimler. The companies of Mercedes and Porsche are close geographically, and also share the Schwabian work ethic

Left

Because the cars were hand-built, production was limited; less than 2500 were built each year, at the rate of only twelve per day. These standards, naturally, do not come cheap: £50,000-plus was the tag on UK models, even though they retained LHD. However, a finer four-door saloon for civilised speed and with more of that 'feel good' factor has – arguably – yet to be devised...

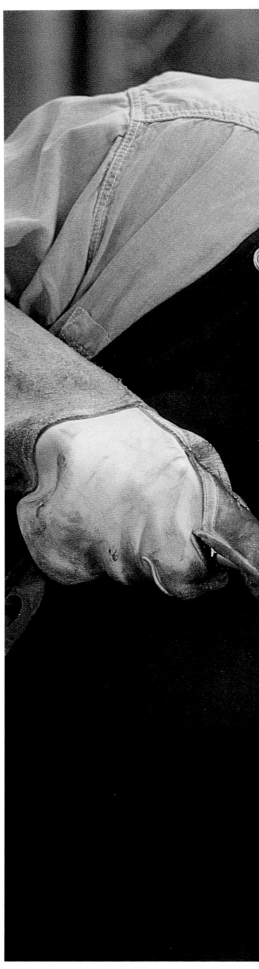

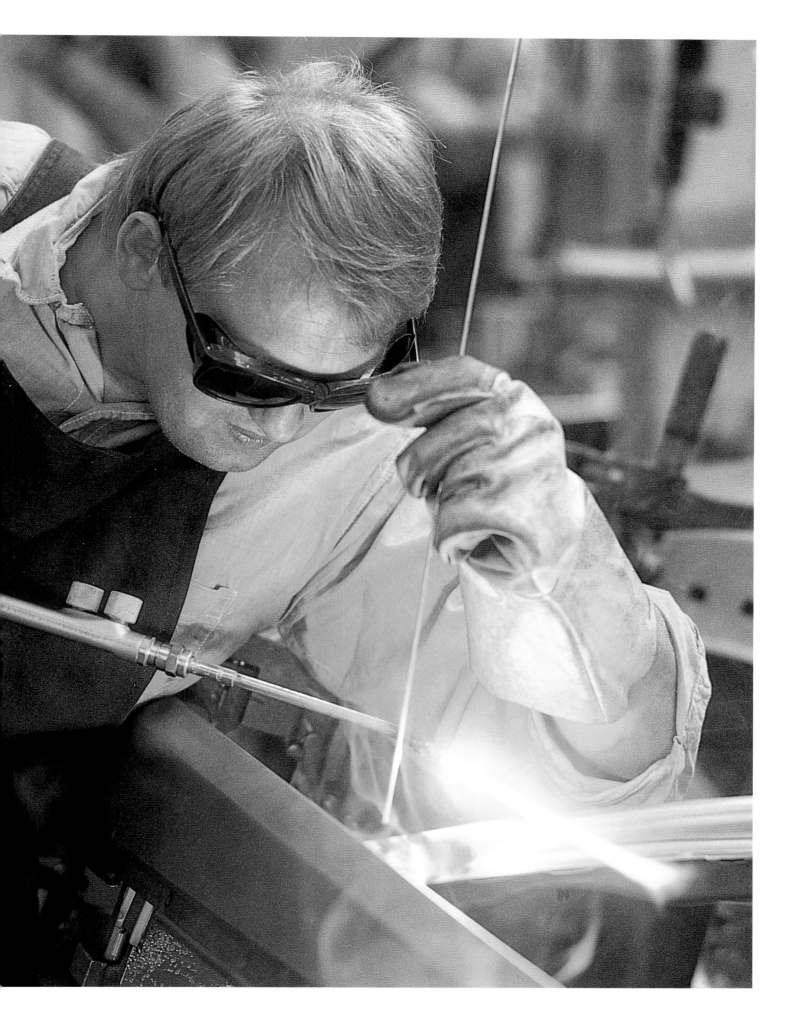

Details, Details

This book did not set out to be a catalogue for Mercedes tuners or Mercedes accessories. There are many other companies, large and small, dedicated to the altering of motor cars in general, and Mercedes in particular.

The firm of Lorinser, for example, which is situated at Fellbach, west of Stuttgart. Their enormous glossy catalogue tells of a myriad styling versions and facelifts, some designed specifically for the US market. Lorinser's philosophy is described on the opening pages in four languages. 'The best or nothing at all' – a motto the company have adopted from the founders Gottlieb Daimler and Karl Benz, says it all. Take a good product to begin with, add the personal touch, make it all fit together well and harmoniously, utilise the latest technology and the best craftsmanship, and you will have the automobile of your dreams. Lorinser are happily able to number successful Formula 1 and rally drivers and engineers among their customers. The design is in the detail.

There are companies specialising in one item, and there will certainly be one to fit your Mercedes. Magazines are filled with customising paraphernalia, from the most professionally engineered turbo system to the most questionable piece of chrome trim. You have probably read of the anguished (but restrained) reactions of Rolls-Royce management when they hear of the Spirit of Ecstasy being replaced by, say, a flying pig: but the customisers reviewed here seem to have a good relationship with the source of their livelihoods. Whatever your taste and style may be, somewhere there is your ideal Mercedes.

In addition to the more usual Mercedes models that attract the customiser, Lorinser turn their attention to the less usual. They provide custom paintwork and specialised accessories for the G-Wagen, spoiler/bumper units with integrated extra headlamps for Mercedes vans and motorhomes, and modifications for older models as well

The sporty touches that are an integral part of Lorinser's philosophy; the completion
of a high-class automobile with a personal touch

Wide tyres and low-slung suspension, along with aerodynamic spoilers front and rear plus side skirts, optimise the roadholding and give a sporty feel. In addition to Pirelli, Lorinser also fit Dunlop and Goodyear tyres — horses for courses. The company provide a wide range of light-alloy wheels, plus locking nuts to ensure they stay on the Mercedes for which they were purchased

Above

Automechanika, the annual fair for tuners and accessorisers of all makes and all marques, is held at the Frankfurt Messe complex. Inspecting all that chrome and leather can be a wearying business, as this gentleman found when he got as far as the Rusta stand

Right

The car is the star – and on a well-lit stand, the three-pointed star shines as bright as all the rest of the polished chrome

Above

Rusta advertise extravagant bodywork and styling – and director Herr Stauber behaves suitably extravagantly to match

Above right

KLS was formed in 1992. Their aim, as Mercedes specialists, is to supply items that are not generally available for the cars. They aim for technical innovation, but sensibly conceived and fitted, always remembering that a Mercedes is a Mercedes, whatever may be added. The cars should be personalised with this in mind. KLS supply tuning kits and complete engines, including turbochargers for the diesel cars; in addition, sports exhausts and suspension, spoilers and both interior and exterior accessories

Right

At Automechanika, Eris Car Design show a luxurious wood interior which typifies their range. They also manufacture metal wing covers, and accessories worked in chrome, steel and brass

Previous pages

Adrian Towland, Managing Director of Path Group, with his 1989 Mercedes 300SL.
The car has been fitted out with state-of-the-art audio equipment by Sound Science
from Iver in Buckinghamshire

Right

The boot contains a Punch 40 DSM amplifier by Rockford-Fosgate, plus an
Audiophile 10-inch 4ohm sub-bass speaker

Above

The doors are fitted with Audiophile 614 kits; 6-inch mid-range and 1-inch dome
tweeters with passive two-way crossovers. They produce a true 20 watts per channel,
with no distortion. Everything is controlled by a Nakamichi CD701

Left

Sound Science completely rebuild the door panels to accommodate the speakers. The result is smooth, integrated and unobtrusive

Above

...or if the sublime 600 doesn't take your fancy, how about the ridiculous

Above

Following in the tradition of the 600 Limousine of the 1960s and 1970s, this stretched 600 SEL can be kitted out with all the essentials of the office on the move. Enough room to hold a board meeting; enough panache for the most up-market arrival you could wish for. The chauffeur is unlikely to complain either

Right

Whatever your taste in customisation, the Mercedes gets the bouquets as an ideal base vehicle; not for nothing does the badge contain the laurels of Benz and the star of Daimler – patriarchs of the automobile

Overleaf

Discretion isn't everything, however; overstating your case is not a crime!